beat stress!
the exam handbook

Crabtree Publishing Company
www.crabtreebooks.com

Crabtree Publishing Company
www.crabtreebooks.com

Author: Anita Naik

Editor: Lynn Peppas

Proofreaders: Adrianna Morganelli
Crystal Sikkens

Project coordinator: Robert Walker

Prepress technician: Margaret Amy Salter

Production coordinator: Margaret Amy Salter

Project editor: Victoria Garrard

Project designer: Sara Greasley

With thanks to Dr. Melissa Sayer

Picture credits:

Sara Greasley and Hayley Terry: p. 9 (bottom left),
17 (bottom), 18 (bottom), 25 (top), 35 (bottom), 45
Jupiter Images: Polka Dot Images: p. 33;
Purestock: p. 30
Shutterstock: p. 1, 2, 4, 5, 6, 7, 8, 9 (top and bottom
right), 10, 11, 12, 13, 14, 15, 17 (top), 18 (top), 19,
20, 21, 22, 23 (top), 24, 25 (bottom), 26, 27, 28, 29,
31, 32, 34, 35 (top), 36, 38, 39, 40, 41, 42, 43, 44

Every effort has been made to trace copyright holders,
and we apologize in advance for any omissions. We
would be pleased to insert the appropriate acknowledgments
in any subsequent edition of this publication.

Library and Archives Canada Cataloguing in Publication

Naik, Anita
    Beat stress! : the exam handbook / Anita Naik.

(Really useful handbooks)
Includes index.
ISBN 978-0-7787-4387-3 (bound).--ISBN 978-0-7787-4400-9 (pbk.)

    1. Test-taking skills--Juvenile literature. 2. Study skills--Juvenile
literature. 3. Test anxiety--Juvenile literature. I. Title. II. Series: Really
useful handbooks

LB3060.57.N33 2009   j371.26   C2008-907873-X

Library of Congress Cataloging-in-Publication Data

Naik, Anita.
  Beat stress! : the exam handbook / Anita Naik.
    p. cm. -- (Really useful handbooks)
  Includes index.
  ISBN 978-0-7787-4400-9 (pbk. : alk. paper) -- ISBN 978-0-7787-
4387-3 (reinforced library binding : alk. paper)
  1. Test-taking skills--Juvenile literature. I. Title. II. Series.

LB3060.57.N35 2009
371.26--dc22

                              2008052357

Crabtree Publishing Company
www.crabtreebooks.com   1-800-387-7650

Published in Canada
Crabtree Publishing
616 Welland Ave.
St. Catharines, Ontario
L2M 5V6

Published in the United States
Crabtree Publishing
PMB16A
350 Fifth Ave., Suite 3308
New York, NY 10118

contents

study methods

No one has ever taught me how to study—what should I do?

When it comes to studying, the good news is there is no right or wrong way to do it. How you review is largely a case of what technique suits you best, as well as the kind of **exam** you're taking— **practical**, **multiple choice** questions, or essays. Know what you're facing to find the right technique.

Trial and error

To find the technique that suits you best think about how you usually remember important facts.

- Are you someone who works on repetition—for instance saying things aloud, or reading something over and over until it sinks in?
- Or are you someone who needs to take notes, highlight key points, and then work on remembering those through repetition (known as active reading)?
- The only way you'll ever know for sure is to try a few different methods and then test yourself to see which one has helped you to absorb the most information in the most efficient way.

Note-taking and re-reading don't work for me—help!

Give **mind maps** or spidergrams a try.

- To create a mind map, you literally draw a diagram with your central theme in the middle of the page and then attach all the important links, facts, patterns, and themes to it using arrows or "spider legs."

- This then allows you to soak up the information as a whole picture and remember important information more effectively.

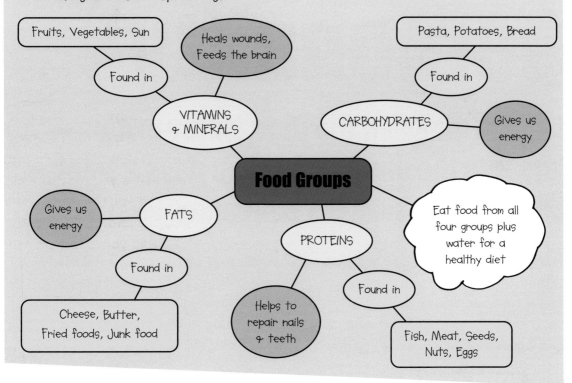

Fruits, Vegetables, Sun — Found in — VITAMINS & MINERALS

Heals wounds, Feeds the brain

Pasta, Potatoes, Bread — Found in — CARBOHYDRATES — Gives us energy

Food Groups

Gives us energy — FATS — Found in — Cheese, Butter, Fried foods, Junk food

Eat food from all four groups plus water for a healthy diet

PROTEINS — Helps to repair nails & teeth — Found in — Fish, Meat, Seeds, Nuts, Eggs

Stress buster

Having an allotted study station somewhere in your home helps you to concentrate better and study for longer.

know your study personality

I like to study all the time for my exams— late into the night and seven days a week— but my mom says it's unhealthy. Who's right?

Exams are more like a marathon than a sprint, which means you need to take it slow and steady to ensure you make it through without becoming ill. This means that even if you're studying within your own limits you still need time off, not just for a mental break but to allow your mind to absorb information and for your body to get a chance to relax.

Why not try...

Studying with friends. This can help if you're easily distracted as it can help you to focus, but only if you make sure your study group is made up of at least two friends who are more studious than you.

I'm someone who finds it hard to start studying—what should I do?

- It's always possible to find something more interesting to do than studying.
- This means the only way to break this habit is to be strict with yourself.
- Even if you're not the organized type, stick to a **study timetable** that structures your time so you don't procrastinate and get distracted.

What's your study personality?

Knowing what kind of student you are can help stop you stalling when it comes to studying.

In order to study do you:
a) Need to have everything super organized?
b) Need a deadline, i.e. the exam is tomorrow?
c) Need people to tell you you're going to do well?

Answers

If you answered:
a) You are a perfectionist at heart. A study timetable is an essential tool for you.
b) Anxiety is your motivator so set yourself daily deadlines as an incentive.
c) You're reliant on others for confidence boosting. Set up study groups with friends to keep your esteem up during study periods.

how to concentrate

I can't concentrate and find myself daydreaming or checking my emails and texts. How can I make myself study?

Studying for an exam is tough because, compared to how you usually study at school, it's a completely different way of working. This means it's easy to be sidetracked, no matter how determined you are.

- Make sure all distractions—cell phones, email, phones, TVs, games consoles—are well out of reach and view.

- Study in short bursts of ten minutes and work your way up to 20 minutes, then 45 minutes.

- Once you reach your goal of 45 minutes give yourself a short five-minute break. This will help to maintain your concentration levels and allows for information to sink in.

Highs and lows

I start studying first thing but after lunch I can't focus and the words don't make sense. What should I do?

- To study well, pay attention to your body's natural energy highs and lows.
- If you wake up full of energy this is your best time to study. By lunchtime your body will be hitting its natural low.
- Come alive after 6pm? Then this is your key time to work.

Did you know?

Research shows some people concentrate better with background noise or music, while others need quiet. Find out what works best for you.

Top study tip

In one study 200 students were helped through their exam and study period by eating bananas at breakfast, break time, and lunch in a bid to boost their brain power. Research showed that the potassium-packed fruit assisted learning by making the students feel more alert.

your studying timetable

I have loads of exams to study for—how do I draw up a study timetable?

A timetable may seem like a waste of time, but knowing what you need to study and how long you have to study will go a long way toward helping decrease exam pressure and **stress**.

1) Look at your **exam timetable** and make a list of all the topics you need to study and in what order.

2) Divide each day you have to study into morning, afternoon, and evening sessions of about three hours each i.e. 9am–12pm, 1pm–4pm, and 7pm–10pm.

3) Estimate how long it will take you to **review** each topic and allocate an appropriate number of sessions to each subject.

Remember to:

- Give more time to subjects you find difficult and schedule these for when you feel freshest.
- It can help to follow a hard subject with a subject you like as this will help keep your motivation going.
- Leave an hour at the end of each day for a study session of what you have reviewed. Repetitiom improves understanding and memory.
- Ensure your day has regular breaks. It can be hard to switch between subjects so schedule breaks in between.

I only ever stick to my timetable for a week and then give up.

- A revision timetable (see the example at the bottom of the page) is only a guide to help you stay organized.
- If you find you slack off for a few days don't be afraid of amending it. It's better to change a timetable than give up on it altogether.
- If however, you can't keep it up, it could be that your timetable is too rigid and needs rewriting.

Day	Morning 9am-12pm	Afternoon 1pm-4pm	Evening 7pm-10pm (1 hour review)
Monday	MATH: Equations (2 hours) ENGLISH: Poetry (1 hour)	SCIENCE: Forces (3 hours)	MATH: Averages
Tuesday	GEOGRAPHY: Weather	SCIENCE: Digestive system (2 hours) History: Columbus (1 hour)	HISTORY: Civil War
Wednesday	MATH: Decimals	ENGLISH: Grammar	SCIENCE: Pollution (1 hour) Watch TV!
Thursday	GEOGRAPHY: Tectonics (2 hours)	SCIENCE: Nutrition	Practice essay-writing
Friday	MATH: Algebra (2 hours) ENGLISH: Writing short stories (1 hour)	HISTORY: World War I	GEOGRAPHY: Tourism research
Saturday	Morning off — tennis	GEOGRAPHY: Coastal regions	SCIENCE: Periodic table
Sunday	ENGLISH: Punctuation	HISTORY: Titanic research	Evening off — cinema!

study tips

Whether you're studying for written or practical exams or coursework, studying in an organized and rational way can help you retain information more easily.

What are the best studying tips?

There are numerous ways to study and review, but psychologists believe the best tried and tested way is to—Read, Reflect, Recite, Review. This means:

- **Read** all your notes
- **Reflect** and highlight what key points you need to know
- **Recite** this information back to yourself using simplified language
- **Review** the chapter again to make sure you have remembered the information you need.

It's not the quickest way to study, but it's a guaranteed way to retain information and understand your work.

Will past exam papers help me?

It's always worth looking at and practicing with past exam papers. Not only will they help you to see how your exam will look on the day, but they will also give you a feel for how the questions are phrased. They are also a good way to practice timed answers so on your exam day you are able to divide up your time appropriately.

Top five research pitfalls

Research is essentially a method of going into your subject in a more complete way. When it comes to studying and your exams, researching can help you to answer questions in more depth and also be more prepared. When doing research be sure to avoid the following:

1) Taking everything you read (especially on websites and in study aids) as truth and fact

2) Copying what you've read and viewed on websites and in your schoolbooks and passing it off as your own work (known as plagiarism)

3) Only researching one person's view on a subject

4) Leaving your research to the last minute

5) Researching too much and becoming overwhelmed by the information

Did you know?

Education watchdogs have called for exam papers and coursework to be scanned by specialist computer software to crack down on internet plagiarism.

cramming

I read my exam timetable wrong and in two days I have a subject I haven't even started studying for—how can I cram for it?

Cramming for exams should be avoided at all costs and should only be used as a last resort because it's difficult to take in a large amount of information in a short period of time. Having said that, sometimes you may have no choice.

- If your time is limited, bear in mind it's too late to learn everything. Your best bet is to focus on areas that you know something about and areas you've been advised are key to this subject.

- As you have no time for details, work on knowing three to five things about each key idea and study these in enough depth to get by.

I've left all my studying too late. I'm now working until the very early hours every night but still can't remember anything.

There's cramming and then there's doing yourself an injury. Working all night, and depriving yourself of sleep is bad news for your health, and bad news for your memory, which of course is bad news for your exams. The solution is to cut back on the hours, get enough sleep, and start again when you feel alert and able.

Did you know?

To learn, we have to transfer information into long-term memory: cramming only places info in short-term storage where it's erased very quickly.

Top study tip

If you have forgotten to study a key point, reading it just before you go into an exam will place it in short term memory for instant use.

coursework, presentations, and practicals

Exams are about more than writing a test, which is why many courses now include coursework, presentations, and practicals as part of the examination process. These examine a variety of elements such as verbal skills alongside memory and understanding.

Presentations and practicals

- Practice literally makes perfect when it comes to this kind of exam so have at least two timed practice runs to give you a feel for what it's going to be like.

- Rehearse in front of an audience to get feedback or videotape yourself.

- During your actual exam, listen actively to the question and always answer with more than a "yes" or "no," using at least two points to illustrate your answer.

- Don't be afraid to ask to start again if you fall over your words.

I'm very behind on my coursework and the deadline is approaching—what do I do?

- Coursework is designed to be done over an academic period or year. It's pretty impossible to cram for it.

- This means if you're seriously lagging behind, you have to confess to your teachers.

- You may be given an extended deadline or offered the chance to rewrite your coursework, as long as you pass the exam that goes with it.

Did you know?

Practicing for presentations in front of the mirror, or talking to an empty chair in front of you, can also help you get used to public speaking and improve your body language.

Top essay-writing tips

1) Take a few minutes to make an essay plan. This is so you can ensure your essay is logical, i.e. what you're saying is clear and makes sense.

2) Write an introduction and conclusion. These should bookend your essays. The introduction should set out what you plan to do and the conclusion should summarize your main points.

3) Ensure you have answered the question. Sometimes the best written essays fail because they simply haven't answered the question.

4) Make sure all your points are backed up with evidence or quotes.

what is stress?

I can't sleep, I'm eating too much and I am having these terrible headaches—is this stress?

Stress is our body's normal response to challenge, threat, or excitement. A little bit of stress can spur us on to do better, but too much stress affects not only our energy but also the way we think and how we feel.

Exam stress can hit you in a number of ways

- Physically you could feel sick, go off food or eat all the time, have sleeping problems, experience headaches, and stomache aches.
- Emotionally you could feel tearful, anxious, irritable, angry, and depressed.
- The way to deal with your symptoms is to talk about your fears with someone who understands and can help you put them into perspective.
- Teachers, parents, doctors, and online counselors are all good for this and can help to both alleviate your stress and help you manage it more effectively. See page 47 for further information.

Is there something I can take to stop me from feeling so stressed?

- The trouble with pills is that they have side effects.

- Things that claim to relax us often affect our concentration and slow us down. Now is not the time to experiment.

- That goes for herbal remedies and anything from the doctor too.

- While doctors can help with more serious exam anxiety, it's important to remember that a small amount of exam stress is not only normal but also expected.

Stress buster

If someone else's high expectations are adding to your exam pressure, it's important to tell them how it's making you feel.

Did you know?

Students who are stressed are more prone to colds and other infections. Daily exercise and healthy eating can provide a buffer against this.

Who said that?

"Basically I took ten minutes out to dance every few hours! Kept my spirits up!"

Lily Cole, model and Cambridge University student

19

staying healthy while studying

I've always been a junk food addict. Will improving my diet really help my exam grades?

A balanced diet is essential for studying because a diet rich in protein, vitamins, and minerals not only boosts brainpower but helps keep your energy levels constant. The super foods for exams are:

- **Oily fish**—rich in brain-boosting omega 3s (eat three times a week)
- **Berries**—rich in antioxidants that help your brain cells (eat once a day)
- **Leafy green vegetables**—high in folic acid that is associated with faster information processing and memory recall.

Is coffee bad when you study?

One coffee may wake you up, but too much coffee overloads your body with caffeine—a stimulant that literally keeps you awake, but also makes you anxious, irritable, and bad-tempered. If you really need a coffee, stick to one in the morning and then have water or juice for the rest of the day.

Top five healthy exam habits

1) Eat three healthy meals a day.
2) Drink one quart (one liter) of water a day.
3) Have eight hours of sleep a night.
4) Exercise for at least an hour a day (you can divide this up into six by ten minute intervals).
5) Take time off every day.

Stress buster

Choose fruit over sugary snacks as they give your body energy in a more even way and don't cause an energy dip.

panic stations

Whenever I think about my exams I feel panicked. My legs go shaky and I feel cold and sweaty. Help!

If your stress levels have gone into overload and you're feeling sheer **panic**, you need to deal with it ... and fast!

What is panic?

Panic is overwhelming fear and anxiety that literally stops you from thinking rationally. It also causes nasty physical symptoms including:
• sweating
• shaking
• dizziness
• a racing heart
• difficulty breathing and choking sensation

It's important to remind yourself that exams don't define who you are, and it's not the end of the world if you don't get the grade you want or need. If you're experiencing physical symptoms and things feel out of control you need to seek help from your parents, teachers, or doctor.

Could your stress level be too high?

Here's some signs you may be worrying too much:

- You have little patience
- You're on the verge of tears or anger all the time
- Your appetite has changed
- You can't relax and your heart starts racing
- You feel breathless and panicky
- You can't sleep and wake up constantly feeling you've forgotten something important. Or the other extreme, you sleep too much.

Did you know?

When your body goes into panic mode you can forget to breathe. The next time you feel it happening, take a long slow breath in through your nose and then slowly exhale. It will instantly calm you down.

It happened to me!

"I'm not an organized person and hate timetables but the only way I can stay focused for exams and keep calm is to have a plan that tells me what I have studied, what I am going to study and when I need to study it by. Without it I am lost."

Melissa, 14

dealing with stress

I am so scared about failing my exams that I feel stressed all the time. I go to sleep thinking about it and wake up with it on my mind.

Establishing what is causing your stress is essential if you want to overcome it. One way to alleviate exam stress is to get your fears into perspective. Exams are important, but failing them isn't the end of the world. If you don't do as well as you'd hoped you can take them again. Your exams do not dictate whether you are a good or a bad person, or whether you are a success or failure in life.

Parental pressure

My parents' stress about my exams is stressing me out big time. It makes me want to give up just to annoy them.

Parental expectation is often at the root of a lot of exam stress, especially if you have parents who are always on your case suggesting you work harder. If this is happening to you, explain how they're making you feel. Tell them what you find encouraging, and what you don't! It might also help to show them that you have a revision plan and that you're in control so they can relax. Don't purposefully do badly to get back at them though—the only person who'll suffer is you.

Five things that make exam stress worse

1) Over-studying
2) Other people's expectations
3) Studying at the last minute
4) Excessive worrying
5) Lack of sleep

Five things that make exam stress better

1) Talking about your fears with parents/teachers
2) Exercising
3) Having time off
4) Reminding yourself that passing exams does not define who you are
5) Not worrying about the future

stress factors

Stress can also arise from other factors around exam time, such as knowing you've left your studying too late, or having parents who don't support your efforts, or even living somewhere that makes it impossible to study.

Help—I feel so stressed out! It's two weeks until my exams and I haven't started studying. What can I do? Every day I just look at all the work and cry.

- Knowing you haven't prepared is a key factor in stress overload, but rather than punishing yourself be proactive.

- Use whatever time you have left to study the subjects you know you have a chance in passing. It may not give you a great overall score, but at least you'll have a few exams under your belt.

- Be honest. Tell your parents and teachers you haven't done enough work, and that this time round you're not going to do well. Preparing them for the worst will alleviate the stress and fear of what's going to happen after the exams.

- Lastly, learn from your mistakes. So you didn't study this time, but next time round change your ways.

Finding support

I have three younger siblings and the house is so noisy I can't study. When I complain to my parents they just say exams aren't important. What can I do?

While exams may not be important to your parents, they are to you, so if your parents are unsupportive find a mentor who will support you. Try a teacher or a relative, and at the same time find a place to work that's quiet. Try some of the places below (see "Alternative places to study") or talk to your teachers and see if there is an empty classroom or place at school you can use.

Alternative places to study

- Your local library
- A friend's house
- A relative's place
- In a cyber café
- In the park

Top five causes of teen stress

1) Noise
2) Tiredness
3) Hunger
4) Thirst
5) Fear

pre-exam nerves

My exams are in two days and even though I've studied I feel really anxious.

Everyone gets nervous before exams, but there are ways to get your anxiety under control.

- The way to keep on top of pre-exam nerves is to express your fears to parents and teachers so that you stop them going round and round in your head.
- Let parents and teachers reassure you that you'll be fine and make sure that in the days up to your exams you eat properly and get enough sleep.
- Lastly, think positively. Studies show this not only motivates you on the day but can also improve your marks.

Whenever I think about my exams I feel sick with nerves, what can I do?

To get your nerves instantly under control:

Step one: close your eyes and breathe out through your mouth.

Step two: slowly breathe in through your nose imagining cool blue air flowing through your body and inflating your stomach.

Step three: slowly breathe out through your mouth imagining the same air leaving and deflating your stomach as you go. Repeat three times.

Instant calming tips

1) Think that by this time tomorrow your exam will be over.

2) Visualize your favorite and most relaxing place.

3) Remind yourself of your last big achievement (it doesn't have to be an exam).

4) Eat a ginger snap! Ginger helps ease mental confusion.

5) Recharge your batteries by doing something you enjoy for an hour.

Did you know?

70,000 teenagers fail to turn up to their exams each year, due to nerves and anxiety. Make sure you're not one of them!

exam day anxiety

I am usually fine until I get outside the exam hall and then all the talk outside sends me into a panic.

Exam day anxiety can cause more than panic. Let it get out of control and it can ruin all your hard work.

- To make it through the day remember to breathe, relax, and then get working.

- The worst thing you can do before an exam is to indulge in a pre-exam analysis of what you've studied and what you haven't with your friends. It's a guaranteed way to make you anxious and will send you into a panic.

- Tell your friends you want to talk about other things or simply turn up five minutes before you go in to avoid these discussions.

- On your journey in, practice some positive visualization (whereby you visualize yourself sailing through the exam with ease).

- Or turn on your MP3 player and listen to some calming music to help you relax and get ready.

Essential exam info

- The start time of your exam
- The last possible entry time to your exam. This can be up to five minutes before the exam begins.
- The exam venue
- The length of the exam
- The exam tools you need to bring
- The rules of the examination hall (Can you leave when you're done? Do you have to raise your hand to go to the bathroom?)

Pre-exam checklist

- Set your alarm so you can get up in plenty of time.
- Lay clothes out the night before—who wants a fashion moment when you're stressed?
- Make sure you have breakfast.
- Make sure you know the time of your bus/train or how long the walk to the examination hall is.
- Go to the bathroom before you go in.
- Have some water with you.

Stress buster

Breakfast can boost brainpower, making you smarter for the day. A study from the University of Wales found that, on average, students who ate breakfast before taking a test scored 20% higher than those who skipped breakfast.

exam room panic

I always do badly on exams because the minute I read the paper, I panic and can't do it.

It's easy to read an examination paper and let the words freak you out. To avoid exam fright make sure you do the following:

- Start by taking a deep breath and reading the exam paper slowly.
- Even if the questions alarm you, continue reading slowly until you feel your terror subside and the questions start to make some kind of sense.
- Then answer the questions you feel the most positive about, as this will boost your confidence and allow you to feel motivated to tackle the rest.
- Make sure you leave around ten minutes at the end to read through your work for small mistakes.

Is there a guaranteed way to pass an exam?

No, but these tips help every time...

- It sounds obvious but before you write a word always make sure that you have read the exam question properly.
- Nerves can make you read something incorrectly or misinterpret the questions, so always read a question twice.
- Then think "what does the person marking this exam want to know and what's the best way to give them my answer (i.e. which key points do I need to make first)?"

Stress buster

Looking around you during an exam only increases your panic levels. If you're going to look up, simply focus on a point in the distance.

Exam Checklist

- Make sure you're in the right examination hall.
- Always remember to write your name on the paper.
- Double check that you have understood the question.
- Double check your answers.

Did you know?

Lemon balm is known to help students suffering from stress. Put a few drops on a tissue and breathe it in whenever you feel overly anxious during your exam.

physical signs of exam stress

When I have to write essays I get terrible cramps in my hand—help!

Stress during an exam can hit as cramps or headaches, so come prepared with headache tablets, water, and be ready to stretch.

- Cramps in your hand is common during exams and comes from the speed you have to write and the amount you have to do in a short amount of time.
- It also happens because stress makes you grip the pen and press down too hard. This causes your hand to be in a continually clenched position and that causes it to cramp.
- Loosening your grip will help. Stop every 20 minutes for five seconds to waggle your fingers and rotate your wrists.

I get really tired in exams and find by my last question I can hardly make it through to the end.

- Fatigue in exams is often caused by dehydration and bad breathing techniques.

- If you find yourself yawning take some deep breaths—it will release oxygen to the brain.

- Not drinking enough will also make you feel tired. Try to take a sip of water every ten minutes (more if the examination hall is very hot). This should sustain you until the end of the exam.

Top exam tip

Being too warm in an exam can make you sleepy and lethargic. Best to wear less clothes and bring a jacket in case you get cold.

Did you know?

Sitting hunched up and stooped over stops blood from reaching the brain. In between exam questions, make sure you sit up (pull your stomach in), roll your shoulders back and forward gently and stretch your neck from side to side.

memory loss

In my last exam I got total memory loss and couldn't remember anything. What if it happens again?

Memory loss is a common symptom of nerves and panic. If you allow yourself to calm down (try the breathing exercise on page 29) you'll find that information will come back to you.

- The way to avoid memory loss in an exam is to write down the key information you can instantly recall before you even read the exam paper.

- This way you will always have key points to feed off in case the exam causes you to literally forget what you know.

- Once you've done this, read the exam questions, and as you read focus on what you know (rather than what you don't).

- This will prevent you feeling anxious about difficult questions and stop your stress levels rising to the point where you forget everything.

Any tricks for helping with memory loss?

Total memory loss is rare in exams but if you really can't recall anything try these memory tricks:

1) Try to "picture" the information you need, for instance if you're trying to remember relevant episodes in a novel/play, visualize the book playing out as a film and use this technique to try and pull information.

2) If you're trying to remember a theory or equation try to "see" the information or hear it being said aloud. Both techniques can help your brain to release information more easily.

Did you know?

Eating foods that contain B vitamins such as beef, milk, and cereals in the weeks up to your exams can help improve your memory and concentration levels.

It happened to me!

"I've always been good at French but in my **oral** exam all my studying went out of my head and I started to panic. Luckily the examiner saw what was happening and told me to take three deep breaths and have a drink of water. Just doing that stopped my panic. Once I calmed down it all started to come back to me."

Tina, 16

post-exam analysis

My friends answered differently than me in my last exam and now I'm worried I got everything wrong. What should I do?

Avoiding post mortems after you have written an exam is the key to feeling positive and energized.

- It's important to remember that once you have taken an exam there is nothing you can do, so don't agonize over what's already in the past.

- Don't indulge in a post-exam analysis of questions with friends, don't have a debate about what you feel were the right and wrong answers, and don't play the guessing game with your mark/score.

- After your exam all you should do is take a well-deserved break, grab something to eat, and then think of the next exam that's ahead of you.

Is there anything I can do after an exam to help myself in the next one?

Looking at your examination strategy and how well you worked during the exam can improve your effort in the next one. Ask yourself:

1) Did I manage my time well during the exam?

2) Did stress get the better of me?

3) Was I as well prepared as I could have been?

Knowing these answers can help you be better prepared in your following exams.

Did you know?

Studies show that girls tend to underestimate their exam scores, while boys tend to overestimate!

Stress buster

If you have exams back-to-back make sure you stretch. Stretching out tired muscles, especially in your shoulders, back and neck, helps release tension. It also improves blood flow to the brain, helping you to think faster and remember more.

I have another exam but am too tired too study anymore.

Motivation doesn't necessarily mean more studying. If you're tired the very best thing you can do is have a good night's sleep. By all means look over your notes before bed, but forget cramming. Instead, have a hot bath, eat a good dinner, relax, and go to sleep. Fatigue can kill your marks quicker than lack of preparation.

results—keep perspective

I feel really anxious about my results. How can I calm myself down?

- In the weeks leading up to getting your results it's easy to lose hope and start to imagine the worst.

- Ignore media reports about how exams have got easier or harder. They will just make you worry even more.

- It's natural to feel uptight about your results, but there's a great deal that you can do beforehand to help.

- Start by being prepared for both good and bad news by drawing up a list of contacts you can call upon for support when your results come through.

- This list should include friends who are good in a crisis, and teachers who can advise you on what to do next.

- Finally, remember that worrying, crying, and getting over-stressed achieves nothing whatsoever because your exams are over and done with.

I can't sleep for worrying about my results. Any tips?

- Relax before bed. Give yourself at least 20 minutes where your mind can chill and not be over stimulated. Try a hot bath or listening to music.
- Make sure your room is cool—a lower temperature helps you sleep better.
- Eat, but not too much. A rumbling stomach and an over full one can keep you up. Avoid caffeine too.
- If anxiety is keeping you awake, get up and write down all your worries on a piece of paper. Don't re-read the list, instead throw it away and go back to bed. Literally taking your worries out of your head can help you to stop worrying and sleep better.
- Regular exercise will ensure you sleep better.

I'm not sure what to do—what if I fail, what if I come last— what do I do?

Results are all about options, whether you get the grades you want, perform better than you ever hoped for, or mess up very badly. The first thing to do with the results is not panic if you didn't do as well as you'd hoped. You're not a failure if you don't score well, as exams can always be retaken, and if you're someone who just can't fathom exams, well the good news is there are many other ways to do well in life.

Five ways to take your mind off your results

1) Get a part–time job.
2) Go on vacation.
3) Do volunteer work.
4) Take up a new sport.
5) Ban talking about it with friends.

when things go wrong

My exam results were a complete disaster. What can I do now?

Failing exams is not the end of the world and the first thing to do is not to panic.

- No matter how badly you have done, remember you have choices and don't need to make any rash decisions.
- What's important is to think about what you want to do now.
- You could rewrite your failed exams, change subjects, or change the way you study.
- Be honest with yourself because knowing why you failed is the best indicator of what you should do next.

I feel devastated. I passed but didn't get high enough grades.

Not making the grades you wanted may make you feel like a failure but the fact is you're not. Sometimes we can place too high an expectation on ourselves, so when we don't achieve it we feel that it's the end of the world. Discuss all your options with your teachers and then think about what you want to do next. It may not be a case of retaking, but simply changing direction.

Five famous flunkers

1) Thomas Edison—Inventor of the electric light bulb and motion picture camera dropped out of school after only three months of education.

2) Bill Gates—The co-founder of Microsoft dropped out of university.

3) Albert Einstein—The Nobel Prize-winning physicist, dropped out of high school at age 15.

4) Richard Branson—The self-made billionaire businessman quit school at age 16.

5) Charles Dickens—The author of numerous classics only went to school until age 12.

It happened to me!

"I failed every exam I took at school when I was 16, even when I tried. I studied but couldn't get it. When my results came through I felt sick and really scared but my mom persuaded me to enroll in a computer course at college and it turned out to be my thing. I now have a great job in a telecoms firm with really fantastic prospects. I thought it was the end of the world when I failed but it really wasn't."

Joe, 18

the ten-point de-stress plan

Stress affects everyone, but learn how to handle it and it will start working for you.

1) **Be realistic** Look at what you can do in the time available. It's better to focus on what you can achieve well in the time you have left, than trying to do the impossible.

2) **Have positive expectations** Focusing on the negative only increases stress and anxiety and stops you from doing your best.

3) **Don't look too far ahead** Stress accelerates when you take a scary thought and run with it i.e. imagining that you'll fail and that will make you a total failure for the rest of your life. Live in the present.

4) Give yourself a break Literally and figuratively. While it's important to prepare, it's more important to get the right work/life balance.

5) Eat properly If you feel sleepy, lethargic, anxious or stressed, you need to change your diet for the better.

6) Exercise It oxygenates our brains, sweeps out the cobwebs, and gets us thinking straight. Exercise is very important as it is proven to improve memory and concentration while reducing the physical effects of stress and preventing depression.

7) Remind yourself that you're in control of your life You may have to take exams but it's your choice how well you do in them.

8) Work on your time management skills Often stress accelerates when you haven't divided your time effectively.

9) Prepare, prepare, prepare Fears and anxieties are about the unexpected—so make sure you know exactly what you're facing.

10) Don't let friends stress you out Especially the ones who claim not to study themselves or hint that you're doing it all wrong.

glossary

cramming Trying to study a large amount of material in a short period, typically the day and night before an exam and usually because you've left your studying until the last minute. It can work for one exam, but isn't a recommended way to study for all your subjects

examination A method of assessment to determine your understanding and knowledge of a subject. They usually have a scoring system to determine not only a pass or fail, but how well you have scored

exam timetable Not to be confused with a study timetable, an exam timetable sets out when, where, and how long your exams are, over the examination period

mind maps A mind map is a diagram that links discussion points, facts, and ideas around a central key theme or subject. They are a visual method of remembering facts

multiple choice exams An exam where you are given a question with multiple answers and you have to choose the right one

oral examinations A verbal exam (as opposed to a written one) where you have to verbally demonstrate your knowledge, and your understanding of a subject. Often used in language subjects

panic An overwhelming feeling of fear and anxiety. When this comes on quickly it's called a panic attack. The feeling is often accompanied by physical symptoms such as sweating, heart racing, feeling sick, giddy, or being unable to breathe

practical exams An exam where you have to physically apply and demonstrate your knowledge and understanding of a subject. Often used in science, arts, and design subjects

presentation Unlike an oral exam where you are asked questions, in a presentation you usually have to prepare a short speech on a topic and answer questions on your speech. A presentation should demonstrate your understanding through the way you communicate your knowledge

review This is an active method of studying to help you remember the information you need for your exams. It can involve a number of techniques including note-taking, mind maps, and studying with friends

study timetable A timetable drawn up in relation to your exam timetable

stress Our body's emotional and physical response to pressure from the outside world. It manifests itself in various ways and can escalate if you don't try to bring it under control

further information

www.kidshelpphone.ca
Confidential counselling anytime.

www.focus as.com/Stress.html
A teen's personalized guide to managing stress.

www.kickoutstress.com
A program to help teenagers navigate this difficult part of their lives.

www.imperialcollegehealthcentre.co.uk/exam.htm
A site to guide you through identifying student stress type
and what you can do about it.

www.memoryskills.com
A selection of study aids and information on how stress
affects your mind and body.

www.reachout.com.au/default.asp?ti=1342
Suggestions for managaing exam stress.

index

Printed in the U.S.A. — CG